First Facts™

Why in the World?

Why Do Tigers Have Stripes?

A Book about Camouflage

by Pamela Dell

Consultant:
Dr. Bernd Heinrich
Department of Biology
University of Vermont

Capstone
press®
Mankato, Minnesota

First Facts is published by Capstone Press,
151 Good Counsel Drive, P.O. Box 669, Mankato, Minnesota 56002.
www.capstonepress.com

Library of Congress Cataloging-in-Publication Data
Dell, Pamela.
    Why do tigers have stripes? : a book about camouflage / Pamela Dell.
        p. cm.—(First facts. Why in the world?)
    Summary: "A brief explanation of animal camouflage, including what it is, why animals use it, and different types of camouflage"—Provided by publisher.
    Includes bibliographical references and index.
    ISBN-13: 978-0-7368-6381-0 (hardcover)
    ISBN-10: 0-7368-6381-8 (hardcover)
    1. Camouflage (Biology)—Juvenile literature. I. Title. II. Series.
QL759.D45 2007
591.47'2—dc22   2005037723

Editorial Credits
Jennifer Besel, editor; Juliette Peters, designer; Wanda Winch, photo researcher;
    Scott Thoms, photo editor

Photo Credits
Ardea/D. Burgess, 17; Corbis/Michael & Patricia Fogden, 4; Corbis/Tim Davis, 10 (left); Corel, 6 (top right); Creatas, 8–9; Dave Welling, 6 (top left); DoD photo by Staff Sgt. Bennie J. Davis III, U.S. Air Force, 21; Getty Images Inc./The Image Bank/Daniel J. Cox, 11 (right); Getty Images Inc./Taxi/Gail Shumway, 6 (bottom); Getty Images Inc./Taxi/K. Jayaram, 15; James P. Rowan, 10 (right); Jim Wetterer, 16; Minden Pictures/Fred Bavendam, 18; Minden Pictures/Jim Brandenburg, 14; Minden Pictures/John Eastcott/Yva Momatiuk, 11 (left); Peter Arnold Inc./Secret Sea Visions, 20 (left); Photodisc, cover (both); Seapics/Robert Yin, 20 (right); Shutterstock/Hatem Eldoronki, 5; Tom & Pat Leeson, 12–13

1 2 3 4 5 6 11 10 09 08 07 06

Table of Contents

Where Are the Animals?

The butterfly doesn't see the hungry, hidden mantis. Snatch! Crunch! The butterfly is now the mantis' tasty snack.

All animals have ways to help them catch **prey** or hide from **predators**. Some animals, like the mantis, have **camouflage**. Camouflage makes animals hard to see.

Scientific Inquiry

Asking questions and making observations like the ones in this book are how scientists begin their research. They follow a process known as scientific inquiry.

Ask a Question

Are grasshoppers camouflaged?

Investigate

Begin looking in the grass to find a grasshopper. When you find one, use a hand lens to study the grasshopper's color, shape, and size. Also take a look at the grasshopper's surroundings. Record what you see in a notebook. Finally, read this book to learn how some animals blend in with their **habitats**.

Explain

You see that the grasshopper is the same color as the grass it lives in. You also note that it's hard to spot the grasshopper in a lot of grass. You decide that grasshoppers are camouflaged. Record your findings in your notebook and remember to keep asking questions!

What Is Camouflage?

Camouflage is all about hiding from other animals. With camouflage, animals are hard to spot in their habitats. A broken tree branch might be a woodland owl. Speckles of sun in the forest may be spots on a fawn's back. A big snowball could turn out to be a snowshoe hare.

DID YOU KNOW?
Many moths, caterpillars, and spiders trick predators by appearing to be wet bird droppings.

Why Are Polar Bears White?

When it comes to camouflage, color rules. Many animals blend in so well with the color of their habitats that you can barely see them. A hungry polar bear's white fur blends in with the snow, making it easier to sneak up on prey.

DiD YoU KnoW?
Pug moth caterpillars eat blue, pink, or yellow flowers. Eventually the caterpillars turn exactly the same color as the flowers they eat.

Some animals change color as their surroundings change. In a rocky desert, the horned lizard looks brown. If it moves to lighter sand, its color changes to match.

Many animals change color when the seasons change. In summer, the fur of an arctic fox is brown. But it will be pure white by the time the snow falls.

Why Do Tigers Have Stripes?

Many animals, like tigers, have patterns of stripes or spots to fool predators and prey. Patterns of light and dark break up the outline of the tiger's body. It's hard for prey to see the tiger coming.

13

Why Does That Bug Look Like a Stick?

Disguise is another tricky kind of camouflage. Many animals are easy to see, but they don't look like animals at all. A walking stick looks just like a twig.

Some animals look like flowers or half-eaten leaves. Others have camouflage that makes them look like sand or rocks.

Why Does *That* Bug Look Like a Snake?

Some animals hide by looking like leaves or twigs. But other creatures trick predators by looking like other animals. The hawk moth caterpillar scares away wasps and birds by looking just like the head of a snake.

When this moth opens its wings, two spooky eyes appear. These eye spots make the moth look like an owl. The "eyes" scare predators away.

Leafy sea dragon

Does Camouflage Work Underwater Too?

Underwater animals use every camouflage trick in the book. Leafy sea dragons look just like the seaweed they live in. Sanddabs don't look like anything but sand.

Predators can't eat animals they can't find. Camouflage is a handy trick for survival in the wild.

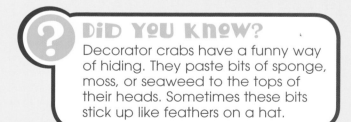

DiD YoU KNOW?

Decorator crabs have a funny way of hiding. They paste bits of sponge, moss, or seaweed to the tops of their heads. Sometimes these bits stick up like feathers on a hat.

CAN YOU BELIEVE IT?

The mimic octopus has an amazing ability to hide. This octopus can actually change its shape to look like another animal. It can take the form of a lion fish, a flat fish, a sea snake, and possibly even a stingray!

WHAT DO YOU THINK?

People have learned a lot about camouflage from animals. In World War I (1914–1918), French soldiers wore dull green and gray uniforms. The uniforms hid them from their enemies in the forests where they fought. What other ways could people use camouflage?

GLOSSARY

camouflage (KAM-uh-flahzh)—the coloring or covering that makes animals, people, and objects look like their surroundings

disguise (diss-GIZE)—to make something look like something else

habitat (HAB-uh-tat)—the place and natural conditions where an animal lives

predator (PRED-uh-tur)—an animal that hunts other animals for food

prey (PRAY)—an animal hunted by another animal

READ MORE

Kalman, Bobbie. *Camouflage: Changing To Hide.* Nature's Changes. New York: Crabtree, 2005.

Stockland, Patricia M. *Stripes, Spots, or Diamonds: A Book about Animal Patterns.* Animal Wise. Minneapolis: Picture Window Books, 2005.

Tildes, Phyllis Limbacher. *Animals in Camouflage.* Watertown, Mass.: Charlesbridge, 2000.

INTERNET SITES

FactHound offers a safe, fun way to find Internet sites related to this book. All of the sites on FactHound have been researched by our staff.

Here's how:

1. Visit *www.facthound.com*

2. Choose your grade level.

3. Type in this book ID **0736863818** for age-appropriate sites. You may also browse subjects by clicking on letters, or by clicking on pictures and words.

4. Click on the **Fetch It** button.

FactHound will fetch the best sites for you!

INDEX